Prepare to be frightened by these terrifying tales from around Somerset

Published by Bradwell Books
9 Orgreave Close Sheffield S13 9NP
Email: books@bradwellbooks.co.uk

British Library Cataloguing in Publication Data: a catalogue record for this book is available from the British Library.

1st Edition
ISBN: 9781909914490

Print: Gomer Press, Llandysul, Ceredigion SA44 4JL
Design by: jenksdesign@yahoo.co.uk
Photograph Credits: iStock and Alamy Picture Library

CONTENTS

INTRODUCTION

Somerset is a wonderfully varied county. Flat fields that were marshes not so long ago (and which become so again after heavy rainfall) give way to beautiful ranges of hills, such as the Quantocks and the Mendips, and to the wild expanse of Exmoor. It also has a wild and lovely coastline, popular with holidaymakers and, previously, smugglers.

The area has been inhabited since the most ancient times. Prehistoric man constructed miles of walkways across the swampy Somerset Levels and buried their dead in mounds on the high hills. A jade hand-axe found by archaeologists beside a trackway proved to be 6,000 years old. There are also many splendid medieval buildings in Somerset: domestic, such as King John's Lodge in Axbridge; military, such as Taunton and Nunney castles; and ecclesiastical, such as the glorious Wells Cathedral, considered one of the finest Gothic buildings in Europe.

Bath, now back in Somerset again after a brief sojourn in Avon, is celebrated for its elegant Georgian architecture. The most popular spa town in England, Bath played host to royalty and the cream of society throughout the 18th and early 19th centuries. Bristol's historic docks launched numerous voyages of exploration in the Middle Ages and from the 17th century became an important hub for the export and import of goods to and from the furthest reaches of Britain's expanding empire. The City of Bristol is now its own unitary authority but for convenience has been included in this book.

There is another side to Somerset that exists beneath the solid landscape of town and country: its legendary landscape.

Somerset is a mystical place, famous for its ancient tales of King Arthur, of Joseph of Arimathea and the Holy Grail, of holy wells and sacred trees, of fairies, witchcraft and magic. The focal point of all this mysticism is Glastonbury Tor, that otherworldly 'island' that rises dramatically out of the Levels, topped off with a ruined medieval church, set there in an attempt to quench its pagan power. The town is a haven for the spiritually minded, encouraged in part by the world-famous rock festival that was launched at the height of 'hippy' culture and the so-called New Age of alternative lifestyles and beliefs.

Bar Cornwall, Somerset is the most Celtic of the English counties. It is thought to have been the 'Summer Land' mentioned in the ancient Welsh collection of folk tales known as *The Mabinogion* and its own rich folklore has a distinctly Welsh flavour. In Somerset history and mystery combine, so it should come as no surprise to learn that it is one of the most haunted counties in the British Isles.

This slim volume can only give a hint of the fascinating variety of Somerset's ghost-lore. However, within these pages you will encounter ghosts of all types: lords, ladies, humble folk, spectral animals, phantom coaches and even a literal ghost train. Many of the county's ghost stories are tied to the doomed Monmouth Rebellion of the 17th century and its aftermath.

Somerset is overly blessed with stunning countryside, quaint old villages and fascinating, historic towns. They are all worth exploring, and you can be sure that one of the county's many haunted sites will not be far away.

AXBRIDGE

Quaint old buildings jostle for attention in Axbridge's attractive little square but the most striking, and arguably the most interesting, is King John's Hunting Lodge. There are two buildings in England going by the name of King John's Hunting Lodge – the other is in Hampshire – yet neither of them were hunting lodges and neither of them have any connection with King John. The Axbridge example dates from about 1500 and was originally the home of a wool merchant. It was recently restored by the National Trust, who reinstated its street-level arcades, and it is now run as a local history museum.

Two quite different but equally charming apparitions have been witnessed in the Hunting Lodge. One of these is a woman in a 'striking' dress of the Elizabethan period. Her favourite haunt is the vicinity of one of the exhibits, a throne-like Mayoral Chair, which dates from the Stuart period. Although this is from a later period in history, the Elizabethan lady enjoys sitting in it.

The Hunting Lodge's other ghost is of a tabby cat. The phantom moggie has been seen in various parts of the building at different times by several otherwise 'hard-headed and disbelieving archaeologists' (to quote *Ghosts of Somerset* by Peter Underwood). It is most often seen in a panelled room on the first floor. It has the habit of pottering in through a closed door, then curling up in a comfortable manner before fading into nothingness.

BATH

The City of Bath is the UK's oldest spa town. Its famous Roman baths were constructed in AD 60 to take advantage of warm springs which emerge from the depths below thc city. The springs were already being enjoyed by the Iron Age tribes living here before the Romans arrived to develop them. The name the newcomers gave to the growing town, Aquae Sulis, may refer to the spirit the Celtic people believed was resident in the spring.

It was in the 18th century, however, that Bath really came into its own. The 'taking of waters' became a health fad in various places, but Bath's spring water was already so celebrated that the city quickly became established as the pre-eminent spa town in England. Its success led to the building of inns and hotels, entertainment centres and elegant housing for the gentry. The Bath Assembly Rooms became the most fashionable location to see and be seen in outside London.

The Assembly Rooms, in Bennett Street, can still be marvelled at today, for they are in the care of the National Trust. It is here that one of Bath's best-known ghosts has been encountered. Because he sports a distinctive style of high-crowned and broad-brimmed headgear, the ghost has become known by the sobriquet of 'The Man in the Black Hat'. The hat has been described as the type a Quaker may have worn in past centuries. The Man in the Black Hat haunts various parts of the Assembly Rooms, particularly the Card Room. He has also been spotted outside, strolling between Portland Place and George Street or making his way down Saville Row towards the Assembly Rooms. On these occasions, he is seen wearing a black cloak as well as his titular hat.

Ghosts are also to be found in a number of Bath's most historic streets, including those lined with its famous neoclassical houses dating from the Georgian and Regency periods. The majority of these homes were designed by architect John Wood the Younger out of the mellow, golden Cotswold Stone. His most spectacular achievement is the Royal Crescent, a sweeping arc of thirty houses (the middle one now a hotel), which was built between 1767 and 1774. Its iconic Georgian frontage has barely changed since it was constructed. A spectral carriage has been observed in the Royal Crescent. It is seen waiting outside, or swiftly departing from, Number 11. This is supposed to be the ghost of the coach which carried away the daughter of the house and the playwright Richard Brinsley Sheridan when they eloped in 1773.

An old illustration of Bath during the 18th century, during its heyday as a spa town. Many of Bath's ghosts date from this period. iStock

John Wood's father designed The Circus, a ring of Palladian houses which serves as a hub from which several of Bath's grandest streets fan out. According to David Brandon's *Haunted Bath*, there was a haunted house in The Circus, appropriately enough Number 13. In the 1950s, renovation work kicked off paranormal activity in the basement flat in Number 13. Objects would be found to have moved overnight, sometimes to other rooms, and pot plants developed the eerie habit of swaying in non-existent breezes. The lady owner was repeatedly woken up by the sounds of someone moving around her bedroom at night, but no one was ever visible. Her housekeeper, however, did see an apparition on more than one occasion, that of an elderly woman in a long grey dress.

The elder John Wood lived in Queen Square and was at the centre of a mild scandal when he invited to move in with him a much younger unmarried woman named Frances Braddock. Frances was a well-known character in Bath, a popular socialite and inveterate gambler. She joined Wood's household in Queen Street after a run of bad luck at the gaming tables left her with enormous debts. Wood was an important personage in Bath and regularly invited the cream of society to his house for parties. At these events, Frances – or Sylvia, as for some reason she was better known – felt her position as a kept woman keenly. Formerly the belle of the ball, she was now treated with indifference or barely veiled contempt. Increasingly depressed, Frances ended up taking her own life. Her unhappy spirit is now said to haunt the house.

Gay Street is one of those elegant thoroughfares that runs down from The Circus and it too has a haunted house. Number 8 is the former home of Mrs Hester Thrale, close friend and later biographer of Samuel Johnson. During her residency, a reception room was known to hum with the voices of invisible people, as if a ghostly soiree was taking place. The apparition of a young man with his hair tied back with a black ribbon was also seen about the house from time to time, but only by men. This latter peculiarity has led to a few jokes in more recent years about the 'gay ghost of Gay Street'.

Number 71, Great Pulteney Street, is haunted by Earl Howe, First Lord of the Admiralty, who spent the last years of his life here, dying in 1799. In full naval regalia, his ghost has been seen striding up and down a room in the house as if he was still on board ship. Another naval man, Admiral Robinson, who by coincidence died the same year as Earl Howe, haunts his former home at Number 20, Henrietta Street.

A phantom coach is said to be seen outside one of the houses in Bath's magnificent Royal Crescent. iStock

An anonymous spook, but one which has been encountered almost as often as The Man in the Black Hat, patrols the Gravel Walk, which leads into Victoria Park. The phantom is described as being of a tall elderly man, dressed in respectable clothing of the late 19th century, with white hair springing out from under his top hat. He has the unnerving habit of following pedestrians, or keeping pace with them, before suddenly walking straight through them!

One of the area's notable landmarks is just outside the city on Bathampton Down. This is the 'Sham Castle' built by 18th-century businessman Ralph Allen, who owned the quarries from which the stone was extracted to face so many of Bath's beautiful houses. The 'castle' is a folly, a castellated frontage with nothing behind it. However, from below it looks like a grand medieval fortress ready to defend the city. So proud was he of the Sham Castle that Ralph Allen is said to return to it in ghostly form on a regular basis.

Nearby something weirder and less identifiable has been seen. David Brandon describes it as 'a large luminous shape … slithering along the top of a stone wall'. It has been observed by many people taking their dog for a walk after dark. One walker said his dogs became aware of its presence moments before he did, their hackles rising as they howled in terror. Only then did he catch sight of the 'definitely not human' thing crawling along the wall. Seconds later the apparition vanished and his dogs immediately became calm.

Arguably the most haunted spot in Bath is in Saw Close. Here the city's famous Theatre Royal stands next door to a pub that is almost as well-known, the Garrick's Head. The pub–restaurant was originally an inn intended to serve the staff, performers and patrons of the theatre. The pub and the main body of the playhouse were built together in 1805 and are further examples of fine Georgian architecture. The Garrick's Head is named after the 18th- century actor David Garrick, who was largely responsible for bringing Shakespeare's plays to a new audience and for rejecting the declamatory style of acting then in vogue in favour of the believable, naturalistic style which we enjoy today. It was originally owned by a contemporary of Garrick's, Richard 'Beau' Nash, a famous dandy who, as Bath's first Master of Ceremonies, helped promote the fledgling spa town into the fashionable resort it became.

The best-known ghost story about the Garrick's Head dates from the time when Beau Nash was running it as an upmarket gambling den. The wine had been flowing freely all night and the charged atmosphere erupted into violence when a cuckolded husband spotted his wife's lover among the crowd. He instantly drew his sword and fell upon his rival in a fury, barely giving him time to defend himself. Stabbing wildly, the outraged husband succeeded in running through the other man, fatally wounding him while his hand was still on the pommel of his undrawn sword.

The murderer made a hasty exit just before his horrified wife arrived on the scene. Her wails of grief and cries of execration against her husband echoed round the room as she cradled her dying lover's head against her bosom. Then, before anyone could stop her, she threw herself out of a window, still screaming. Her screams continue to be heard from the room where she took her life. The shadowy and much less noisy ghost of her doomed lover also haunts the room.

In addition, the Garrick's Head is haunted by the apparition of a gentleman of the Regency period, whom Peter

The Sham Castle overlooking the city of Bath is haunted by its eccentric builder.
iStock

Underwood describes as 'a heavily-built man wearing a long brown wig, a form that makes squeaky footsteps as it moves but leaves no footprints'. Underwood gathered testimony from several former landlords who all reported paranormal incidents in the pub. One witnessed two candles lifting themselves out of their sticks before flying across a room, and another saw an even more amazing feat: a heavy cash register launched itself from the bar and smashed a chair to smithereens. Odd noises and a weird ghostly glow seemed to have been common phenomena in the Garrick's Head at one time.

A ghostly Grey Lady haunts both the Garrick's Head and the Theatre Royal. Some believe she may be the ghost of the woman who threw herself to her death after her lover was killed. Her demise was so full of drama, it's possible she was indeed an actress. At any rate, the Grey Lady's main haunt is the theatre. She is most often seen in a box above the auditorium, but she has also been seen in the lower circle and has been known to wander through the stalls as if the seats are non-existent. On one occasion in 1975, almost the entire cast of a play saw the Grey Lady watching them as they performed on the stage.

The Grey Lady is not the Theatre Royal's only ghost. A spectral doorman haunts the vestibule and a tall, imposing male figure has been observed in the vicinity of the stage. Those who have seen the latter ghost are convinced it is of the great 19th-century actor Sir Henry Irving.

The strangest tale associated with the Theatre Royal, Bath, involves that most benign of creatures, the butterfly. The legend started in 1948 when the then manager, Reg Maddox, died of a heart attack while helping to light a ballet whose backdrop was an enormous butterfly. Shortly before his collapse, a small tortoiseshell butterfly had been seen to land near him. The distressing incident caused the butterfly ballet sequence to be pulled from the pantomime in which it featured. However, a few days before the panto's run, another small tortoiseshell was seen fluttering around backstage, and this was taken to be such a good omen that the dance was reinstated. Since then a butterfly of the same species has been said to appear before any successful run.

Small tortoiseshells hibernate in odd corners of old buildings so it's not too surprising if one or two, disturbed by activity such as the hanging of lights, were seen to flutter about briefly, even in the depths of winter. Nevertheless, the omen of the butterfly at Bath's Theatre Royal has become an established part of theatre-lore and over the years the implication has been made that it is actually a manifestation of Reg Maddox's spirit, bringing his blessing from the other side. This is certainly how actor and comedian Leslie Crowther interpreted his experience of the butterfly phenomenon during the opening performance of a panto in 1979. In his book *The Bonus of Laughter*, he recalled:

'I must say that nothing was further from my mind when I prepared in the wings to make my entrance in the Boxing Day matinee, but then a miracle happened. After Reg Maddox had allowed me sufficient time to establish rapport with the audience he fluttered down from the spotlight in the form of

An early engraving of the Theatre Royal, Bath, haunted by a former actress known as the Grey Lady.

a tortoiseshell butterfly and alighted on my left shoulder! I gently scooped it/him into the wings, meanwhile telling the audience that I would tell them at the end of the performance why I was looking so gob-smacked – which I did. And yes! The pantomime was a big success.'

BRIDGWATER

The most famous 'old boy' of this 'capital of the moors', as it is known, is Robert Blake. Blake was born in 1598 and enjoyed an illustrious career in the British navy. His efforts have been credited by some historians as instigating Britain's eventual dominance of the sea in the 18th century. He was the most important naval commander during the Commonwealth under Oliver Cromwell, and was awarded the title of General at Sea. His former home in Bridgwater is now the Blake Museum and it is said that he haunts the place.

There are a number of haunted properties around Bridgwater. A ghostly form has been seen kneeling in one of the pews in the parish church, and phantom figures wrapped in grey cloaks, or wearing grey habits, haunt the 13th-century archway in Silver Street. There is also a story about a house in the town where disembodied footsteps were often heard in one of the bedrooms. Two young girls who slept in the room were visited by the ghost and were brave enough to talk to it. The spirit revealed to them the hiding place of a hoard of gold, with the result that the household became instantly rich and the house itself ceased to be haunted!

Tradition states that the ill-fated Duke of Monmouth stayed in Bridgwater Castle before the Battle of Sedgemoor in 1685 and his dashing figure is said to still be seen about the ruins.

Monmouth is also believed to have stayed at Sydenham Manor House, a 16th-century mansion most recently used as offices, and here too his ghost has been seen, in the aptly named Monmouth Room. An old building in St Mary Street is supposedly haunted by another figure connected to the Monmouth Rebellion – or rather its aftermath – 'Hanging' Judge Jeffreys. Only the heavy pacing of his footsteps has been heard, however. (For more on the Monmouth Rebellion and ghosts of this period, see the sections on Chard and Sedgemoor.)

Elsewhere, another 'celebrity ghost' has been seen: Alfred the Great. For a period in the 9th century, Alfred found himself virtually marooned in the moors around Bridgwater after the Danes had overrun his kingdom. The muted sounds of steel clashing on steel have occasionally been heard on this stretch of moorland, and they are believed to be the psychic echo of a battle between King Alfred's men and marauding Danes.

BRISTOL

The city of Bristol, now a metropolitan county, is the most populous in south-west England. It has been a major port since at least the 11th century. In the medieval period Bristol was in the top three of the most important English cities after London (along with York and Norwich). The first English-speaking expedition to the New World left from Bristol, in 1499. Earlier in that century there had also been a surprising number of expeditions in search of an entirely mythical island known as 'Hy-Brasil', all of which, needless to say, proved fruitless.

For centuries Bristol's docks were just outside the city walls and these are now preserved as heritage attractions. The new docks are at Avonmouth, closer to the sea. Among the other attractions to be enjoyed at Bristol are two historic ships: the *Matthew*, a replica of the vessel that discovered Newfoundland in the 15th century, and Isambard Kingdom Brunel's mighty SS *Great Britain*. In addition, there is the world-famous Bristol Zoo, an aquarium, and several museums and historic properties around the city, including its modest but beautiful medieval cathedral.

The cathedral dates back to the 12th century but was redesigned and extended up until the 15th century. It is haunted by the apparition of a monk in a grey habit. The Grey Monk is a studious fellow. He makes his way through the cathedral before passing through a blocked-up doorway which leads to a library. In the library itself he has been observed sitting and frowning, as if concentrating on some now invisible work of theology. By rights, his habit should be black, reflecting those worn by the Augustinian order which ran the original priory before it was given cathedral status. However, as Daniel Codd suggests in his *Mysterious Somerset and Bristol*: 'Perhaps, down the centuries, he has faded somewhat!'

All Saints' Church in Corn Street is an exact contemporary of Bristol Cathedral: 12th century with additions no more recent than the 15th. At one time the church had a superb collection of books (better than those of the cathedral) and it became the first free library in England. It was in the control of a rich guild and, in addition to its library, it was possessed of a considerable amount of expensive plate. According to legend, when Henry VIII closed the monasteries, his agents also raided All Saints' Church but were unable to find all the valuables they knew it contained. They strongly suspected that

Bristol Cathedral is haunted by a studious monk.
iStock

a hoard of plate and jewellery had been hidden somewhere, but, in spite of an intensive search, were unable to find it.

The shadowy form of a Black Monk has been seen by a number of vicars and worshippers at All Saints' Church. He is thought to be the ghost of the monk who concealed the treasure at the time of the Dissolution and now guards its hiding place. He is most often seen floating down the chancel before disappearing through a wall. The nearby vicarage was also haunted by a monk in a black habit. In addition, mysterious lights and the heavy tread of an unseen presence were encountered about the house.

The Theatre Royal in King Street has been in continuous use as a theatre for more years than any other building in Britain. It was founded in 1766 and now houses the Bristol Old Vic company, an offshoot of the Old Vic in London. Today the playhouse is generally known as the 'Bristol Old Vic' rather than the Theatre Royal. A former dressing room was popularly believed to be haunted by the greatest tragedienne of the Georgian and Regency periods, Sarah Siddons. After years of improving her craft on endless tours round the provinces, in which she may well have performed in the Theatre Royal, Bristol, Sarah had a smash hit as Lady Macbeth at the Theatre Royal in London's Drury Lane. From then on she was the darling of London society and her reputation as a passionate and mesmerising performer of tragic roles became assured.

Sarah Siddons's ghost is said to haunt a number of theatres and also her former home in Baker Street, London. It may perhaps be wishful thinking to imagine that the gentle, female phantom seen drifting round the Bristol Old Vic is another manifestation of this immortal actress. A former dressing room was certainly haunted by someone or something. Ghost-hunter Peter Underwood spoke to an actress who experienced some very peculiar things while she was using this dressing room.

On one occasion the actress entered the room to find it inexplicably in darkness and all its contents, including the costume she was due to wear on stage, scattered all over the place. Then the light in the corridor outside mysteriously dimmed, an unearthly chill descended, and the actress was unnerved to hear the sound of a sobbing woman from an empty corner of the room. She later learnt that one of her dressers had also heard the sobbing on a previous occasion.

The oddly named Llandoger Trow is just across the road from the Bristol Old Vic. This majestic timber-framed inn dates from the 1660s and is named after a type of flat-bottomed barge that was widely used for transporting goods in and out of Bristol Docks. Llandoger (today spelled Llandogo, or in the correct Welsh, Llaneuddogwy) is a Monmouthshire village where many of the trows were built. This venerable hostelry is rather famous. In the 1880s, Robert Louis Stevenson used it as the model for the Admiral Benbow inn in *Treasure Island*. In the early 18th century Daniel Defoe is said to have met Alexander Selkirk, the real-life castaway who inspired Defoe's *Robinson Crusoe*, at the Llandoger Trow.

For many years the Llandoger Trow was haunted by the apparition of small, lame boy. He is thought to have been a young servant of the inn who died here centuries ago. He was most often seen in the yard, where his duties included pumping water into jugs and basins, and in a room above the bar. It's been a while since he was seen but the sound of his soft, limping footsteps are still occasionally heard. Any other odd noises after dark, or puzzling incidents such as the

Bristol's famous Llandoger Trow public house is haunted by a former servant.
iStock

mysterious disappearance of objects or falling of glasses from shelves, continue to be blamed on this harmless little ghost.

Oldbury Court, at Fishponds, was demolished in 1949 after a disastrous fire. In the years leading up to the blaze, scary stories were told about the 17th-century mansion. During the Second World War it was used as a hostel for girls and presided over by a Miss Brownlee, whose London home had been destroyed during the Blitz. Miss Brownlee reported seeing a host of ghosts in Oldbury Court. They included a monk-like figure in a long, hooded cloak; a dumpy little woman, possibly a long-defunct housekeeper; and a group of five women wearing tall head-dresses. On one occasion, Miss Brownlee saw the five female phantoms discussing something in an agitated manner while the 'monk' looked on. Unfortunately, the performance was carried out in dead silence so she was given no idea of what incident the vision might recall.

After dark the distressing sound of a child crying was regularly heard by Miss Brownlee; a child much younger than the girls in residence. Unnerving dragging sounds and unexpected bangs and crashes also disturbed her sleep. The teacher was careful not to mention any of her experiences to her charges, but after a while the girls started to complain of the 'presences' they too had encountered. After the war, the hostel closed and, as stated above, was pulled down not long after.

Today, the extensive grounds of Oldbury Court are accessible to the public and, situated as they are just a few miles from the city centre, comprise a popular haven of peace for Bristolians. The parkland is said to still be haunted by a woman who was unlucky enough to have been struck by lightning while riding her horse across it.

Bristol's most striking landmark is undoubtedly the Avon Gorge, a deep limestone ravine through which the River Avon makes its way to the sea. The gorge is spanned by the impressive Clifton Suspension Bridge built by Isambard Kingdom Brunel. The great Victorian engineer is thought to be the ghost that has been glimpsed from time to time on the bridge. It certainly resembles him: a man in a black frock-coat, a tall hat on his head and a large cigar clamped in his stern jaws as he hurries along. Nearby, on Clifton Down, Leigh Woods also have a haunted reputation. Bloodcurdling screams have been heard shrieking through the trees and dog-walkers have reported that their pets have suddenly gone almost mad with fright at something only they could see.

The Clifton Suspension Bridge is haunted by a figure with a similar bearing to its famous Victorian designer. iStock

One of the most remarkable cases of a haunting in Bristol comes from Hotwells, a suburb to the south of the city, near the suspension bridge. The district takes its name from hot springs, similar to those at Bath, which bubbled up from the ground here. An attempt to exploit the commercial value of these 'medicinal' springs was made as early as the 17th century. A 'pump room' was created but it failed to attract sufficient customers away from Bath. In 1816 it was demolished and replaced with a private home, Hotwells House.

In 1831, a retired lawyer by the name of Wayland moved into Hotwells House, together with his youngest daughter and several servants. Within a year they had discovered that the house was badly haunted. Mr Wayland's son, James, described the haunting to the Revd F.G. Lee, who reproduced the account in his 1885 book, *Glimpses In The Twilight*. James Wayland described how the servants began to be disturbed by unpleasant noises emanating from an empty attic. One of these sounded like someone was being choked to death. One night, the entire household was woken by a rowdy kerfuffle in the courtyard, as if a great crowd of angry men had descended on them. However, the courtyard was found to be empty. On another occasion, intruders were heard yelling on the roof and throwing down tiles into the courtyard below. But again, no one was to be seen; and the roof tiles were undisturbed.

The servants began to see two ghosts around Hotwells House, and they were both very strange. One took the form of a huge dog. The other resembled a monstrous ape! The dry, legal mind of Mr Wayland refused to countenance the idea of ghosts and he believed that the family were the victims of pranksters. Men from the village (as Hotwells then was) were called in to patrol the house after dark but they too heard the strange noises in the attic. Five men saw the apparitions of both the ape and the dog together. James Wayland notes: 'They seemed to come up through a closed grating from a large cellar underneath an outhouse, and to crash out into the darkness beyond the gates of the enclosure.'

Within a year, the Waylands had had enough. They moved out in 1832 and sold Hotwells House to a merchant, but he too found the place unbearable. In an attempt to rent it out, the merchant had the house converted into three cottages, but no one could bear to live in them for long. Hotwells House remained empty for years, falling rapidly into disrepair. The locals avoided the place after dark, but even after it had been demolished in the 1860s there were occasional reports of spooky things being seen in the field in which it had stood, including 'a huge black dog with a monster riding on its back'!

James Wayland later learnt of rumours that, shortly after it was built, a series of murders had been committed at Hotwells House by highwaymen who used it as a base. This was supposed to explain the haunting, but it hardly explains why the ghosts should have appeared in such a strange guise.

Elliott O'Donnell, a legendary ghost-hunter whose books are stuffed with claims of personal encounters with strange and frightening spooks, was brought up in Clifton. In one of his books he refers to a terraced house in Clifton which was haunted by, among other things, 'a strange-looking figure … evil and grotesque, more like some huge, horrible ape than a human being'. Had one of the ghosts of Hotwells House found a new place to haunt after its demolition?

In the 1830s, the Hotwells district of Bristol was a village centred on the remarkably haunted Hotwells House. Clifton Suspension Bridge can be seen in the background spanning the Avon Gorge. iStock

BROCKLEY

Brockley Court is the famous haunted house of this large village near Bristol Airport. The 18th-century manor house has now been converted into flats. In the 1930s Elliott O'Donnell received a letter from the then owner of Brockley Court, a Mr Palmer. Enclosed was a photograph of a hawk-nosed man wearing a black skullcap and a white, belted habit or robe and standing in front of a pillar in a panelled room. However, the panelling could be seen through the figure, who was partly transparent. Mr Palmer explained that the photo was taken in the small hours of the morning in a room believed to be haunted by a monk. He had made the exposure after seeing what he described as a 'curious light' in the room.

Thoroughly intrigued, Mr O'Donnell visited Brockley Court and, in the company of Mr Palmer, carried out a vigil in the allegedly haunted room. 'Nothing happened till about a quarter to three, when we saw a faint glow in cylindrical form on the right side of the room,' explained Mr O'Donnell. 'It seemed to emerge from the wall. On the chance of its being anything superphysical, I stood up and asked if there was a spirit present, and if so would it speak, rap, or give some other token. Though we listened intently we could hear nothing. The light vanished after moving some few feet, and nothing further happening, we came away.'

Elliott O'Donnell made further visits to Brockley Court with equally uncertain results. On one of these investigations one member of his team repeatedly saw a 'dreadful figure' looming out of the darkness, but all O'Donnell saw was a dim red light.

Antony Hippisley-Coxe has another tale to tell about Brockley Court. In his *Haunted Britain*, he writes that the manor house was haunted by 'an old woman whose ghost brings madness or death to all who see it'. Perhaps O'Donnell was lucky not to see anything more than a dim light or two! Mr Hippisley-Coxe adds that this frightening phantom only appears once every twenty-six years, however.

The same author states that a spectral carriage, 'driven hell-for-leather', charges down the hill at nearby Brockley Combe. Its appearances are so sudden and alarming that it has caused numerous accidents. This area is also the haunt of the evil Parson Hibbetson. According to the legend, Hibbetson happened upon the local squire, who had been injured in an accident. The squire was carried back to Hibbetson's house and here the apparently pious parson nursed him carefully back to health. The two men became friends and the squire altered his will in Hibbetson's favour – at which point the parson promptly murdered the deluded man.

Peter Underwood adds further ghosts to those haunting Brockley Combe. One is of Dinah Swan, an old woman who was murdered trying to defend her home from burglars. Another is of an unidentified man in black with a white collar. In addition, there is a phantom horseman; a young girl who killed herself at the end of an unhappy love affair; and the strange 'Bounding Ghost', a tall, skinny, ill-defined form that bounces along the lane before vanishing into the trees.

CHARD

Chard is Somerset's highest and most southerly town. It is close to the border with Devon. In 1662 decidedly peculiar phenomena were witnessed here, on three different days. On July 12 two suns appeared in the sky. Two days later, at 10pm, three moons looked down on the town. Then, on July 19, exactly a week after the first appearance, two suns were again in the sky. Were the phenomena early examples of UFO sightings or merely weird weather effects?

You can't go very far into Somerset's supernatural landscape without becoming immersed in the Monmouth Rebellion and its aftermath (see, for example, the section on Bridgwater). James Scott, the First Duke of Monmouth, was the illegitimate son of Charles II and he was determined to take the throne on the king's death. The legitimate heir was his uncle, James, the Duke of York, but his Catholicism made him an unpopular choice for some. Monmouth exploited this anti-Catholic feeling to push forward his own claims, but his plots only succeeded in having him banished from the kingdom.

On Charles's death, Monmouth landed a small force in Dorset and immediately rallied round him a considerable show of support from gentry in the West Country. His rebellion was short-lived, however. After a number of skirmishes, it was soon crushed by the newly crowned James II's army at the Battle of Sedgemoor (see 'Sedgemoor' below).

Following the Rebellion, a top judge, the 1st Baron Jeffreys of Wem, was put in charge of trying rebels and supporters in the south-west. Jeffreys was under orders to make sure no such trouble would occur again, and his response was merciless, hanging hundreds of people for treason, many of whom may have had nothing to do with the uprising. Many innocents found themselves swinging at the end of the rope during what became known as the 'Bloody Assizes'.

One of the Assizes was held at Chard. Jeffreys ordered a dozen men who had joined Monmouth's cause to be hanged from a big old tree on a neighbouring hill, afterwards called Hang Oak Tree. Even to this day, a signpost at the foot of the hill is painted blood red in commemoration of the deed. During the Assizes, Judge Jeffreys lodged at the 16th-century Choughs Hotel. His ghost now haunts the hotel and has been seen crouched in front of the fire or pacing an upstairs room. One witness, a former policeman, described the apparition as 'a nasty old chap'.

Jeffreys isn't the only ghost in the Choughs, however. A man in armour has been seen patrolling a corridor. Apparently a prisoner, he is in chains, with iron restraints on his wrists and feet. His identity is a mystery but the armour suggests he predates the Monmouth Rebellion.

A number of guests have had disturbed nights in one of the bedrooms. They have been woken by whispering and muffled laughter from somewhere in the darkness. The voices appear to be those of women, but no one is ever seen. There is something distinctly sinister about the voices, with more than a hint of malice behind the laughter. Those brave enough to stay in the room long enough to listen have heard one voice rise in pitch above the others. Although the words remain unclear, they have an unmistakeably spiteful tone. The meaning behind this haunting is unknown, but the room opens on to the corridor where the chained figure has been seen. It's possible the whispered conclave is referring to him.

The splendid country house of Forde Abbey has its postal address as Chard, Somerset, but it is actually just over the border in Dorset. Forde started life as a Cistercian monastic house in the 12th century but went the way of all such institutions during Henry VIII's Dissolution of the Monasteries. The abbot at the time of the Dissolution was named Thomas Chard, presumably after the town. He was so heartbroken at being turned out of the monastery that his spirit still haunts the house. He is most often seen in the Great Hall.

This rather benign portrait of Judge Jeffreys belies the ruthless way in which he behaved at the so-called 'Bloody Assizes'. He haunts several places in Somerset and his addiction to executions has created a number of other ghosts.

CHILTON CANTELO

Higher Farm in this village near Yeovil is famous for possessing a 'screaming skull'. There are a number of 'screaming skulls' around the UK, all kept in houses in which there is a tradition that, should the artefact be removed, disturbing paranormal activity will immediately break out, sometimes (but not always) including unnerving screams. The skulls are usually believed to belong to a former owner of the house or to some holy martyr. Sometimes they have turned out to be of prehistoric origin instead, probably unearthed from some nearby burial mound, and therefore nothing to do with the person they are supposed to have belonged to. The keeping of skulls in grand houses seems to link with guardian spirit superstitions dating back to Roman times; or perhaps even earlier, to Celtic 'head cults'.

The Chilton Cantelo skull's provenance, however, is more assured. It belonged to Theophilus Brome, who died at Higher Chilton Farm (as it then was) in 1670. Brome had been a keen Parliamentarian during the English Civil War and was concerned, following the Restoration of the Monarchy, that his body might suffer a similar fate to those of Oliver Cromwell and some of his supporters: namely, that it would be dug up by Royalist fanatics and the head cut off and put on vulgar display. He asked for his head to be removed after burial and kept in the house. When Brome's grave was opened in the 19th century, his skeleton was indeed found to be missing the skull, in support of the story.

Over the years, a number of people attempted to remove the dusty old relic from the house, but were put off from doing so when it emitted 'horrid noises portentive of sad displeasure' (to quote an old source). The most recent attempt took place as long ago as the 1770s, but when the sexton's spade suddenly snapped in half when he'd barely begun to dig the hole that would have received it, he immediately gave up the job as an ill-omened one. Theophilus Brome's skull therefore still resides at Higher Farm, in a neat little cupboard specially constructed for it above a doorway.

An early 20th-century sketch of Higher Farm, Chilton Cantelo, where a skull is reverently kept.

DUNSTER

The gloriously olde worlde village of Dunster is much photographed thanks to its medieval Yarn Market in a square lined with charming old buildings, the entire scene dominated by a castle perched upon a lofty crag. Dunster Castle is open to the public and in the care of the National Trust. Originally a Norman fortress, the gatehouse is the only substantial remnant of its medieval past; most of what we see today was built in the 17th century and then tarted up in the 19th to give it the rather splendid, fairy-tale appearance it has today.

Dunster Castle featured in two civil wars. During the 12th-century Anarchy of Stephen and Matilda, it was first held by Matilda but, after a siege and fierce fighting, was taken by the king. It was a Royalist stronghold during the Civil War of the 17th century and for a long time was successfully defended by a Colonel Wyndham against besieging Parliamentarians. The Roundhead commander became so frustrated by his failure to storm the castle that he dragged Wyndham's elderly mother in front of the cannons and threatened to blast her to kingdom come unless he surrendered. The brave old lady demanded that her son ignore the threat and 'do his duty', shaming the Roundheads into letting her go. Eventually the castle fell and Oliver Cromwell ordered the walls to be demolished.

Several of Dunster Castle's ghosts date from the period of this second siege. The apparition of an old woman in 17th-century costume which stalks the grounds with a haughty expression may well be Colonel Wyndham's indomitable mum. The gatehouse is haunted by a Roundhead soldier. He tends to be seen in the so-called 'Leather Gallery', a chamber hung with rare antique wall-hangings made of leather and showing scenes from the story of Antony and Cleopatra. Odd 'mutterings' have also been heard in this room. Next to the Leather Gallery is a 17th-century staircase down which a 'Grey Lady' sometimes glides.

An unusual and subtle phenomenon, described as the sound of coins chinking together, has also been detected in Dunster Castle. Rather optimistically, it has been connected to King Stephen's siege, when the then lord of the manor continued to mint his own coins despite the battles going on outside.

There are also reports of a former guide to the castle still making unexpected appearances. According to a newspaper interview with property manager William Wake, visitors have from time to time made complimentary remarks about an 'older lady volunteer', even though no one answering her description had been working in the castle. She sounded very much like a lady who had guided people round the castle for many years but who had recently passed away. 'We can only assume it's our old volunteer who pops in every now and again to chat to the visitors,' said Mr Wake.

John Garland, author of *Haunted Somerset*, interviewed a flesh and blood member of the volunteer staff, who told him that a number of people had had spooky experiences in the area of the shop and the old stables. June Copp informed him: 'A previous shop manager told of a man dressed in green that passed the door of the shop and proceeded down the stable block only to disappear without trace. The next shop manager told of a mysterious green light that floated from the front door to the far end of the stable block.' Mr Garland also learnt that ill-defined phantoms have regularly been glimpsed on Bat's Hill, a nearby Iron Age hill fort.

The haunted Gatehouse of Dunster Castle photographed in the days when the castle was still a private home.

DUNSTER, SOMERSET

An early 20th-century postcard of Dunster, showing its medieval Yarn Market, with the castle above.

Another medieval building, rather better preserved and just as interesting as the castle, is the Nunnery in Dunster. Now converted into three, three-storey terraced houses, the Nunnery, as the name suggests, started life as a convent. Today it remains private property. Peter Underwood received a letter from a woman who spent an uncomfortable night in the Nunnery some years ago. She explained that as soon as she and her husband moved into the room, she felt unaccountably threatened. After dark, she became so unnerved that despite the fact there were only single beds in the room, she insisted on sharing one with her husband.

She continued: 'During the night I woke suddenly and saw a figure standing at the foot of the bed. I was not aware of a face, just a white outline of a bareheaded person dressed in flowing robes. I screamed and the shape melted away quickly as if it was a light that had suddenly been turned off.

'My husband saw nothing and thought the whole affair very amusing indeed. The room was quite light and I was not dreaming. I was very wide awake when I saw "it". We never asked about it in the morning when we left, something I have regretted ever since.'

EXMOOR

Exmoor is a former Royal Hunting Forest covering an area of west Somerset and east Devon. The precise area is debatable, depending on whether you include the entire hunting ground as originally drawn up, the remnant of moorland that survives, or the whole of the Exmoor National Park, which also takes in the Brendon Hills, a number of valleys and a stretch of the coastline.

Whichever you choose, Exmoor is a wild and beautiful place, characterised by high heather moorlands and scrubby heath, broken by narrow valleys containing tumbling streams, and interspersed by patches of ancient woodland. It glows golden

An Exmoor pony above the Valley of the Rocks. Phantom ponies are also said to haunt the National Park. iStock

and purple in the autumn and is frequently shrouded in sea-mists which enhance its air of isolation and mystery. Exmoor is also famous for its all-but-wild ponies which freely roam the moor. It's thought that the Exmoor ponies may be the closest breed to wild horses left in Europe.

Not all these ponies may be what they seem, however. There exists an old legend about a ghostly pony on Exmoor called 'Old Tom'. In the old days, when the horses were rounded up, cowboy-style, and driven to market or to the mines, where they would be forced to work as pit-ponies, it was said that Old Tom would emerge from the mists and lead the mares away so that they could not be caught. A ghostly pure white pony is also said to haunt the moors.

On Winsford Hill, an upland heath now managed by the National Trust, a very different phantom animal may be encountered. This is a huge, terrifying black hound with great smouldering eyes the size of saucers. Should a night-bound traveller encounter this spectral beast, he or she should stand stock still; if they advance or try to run away from the hound, they will be cursed. But if they stand and face it down, the hound will slowly fade away, the twin glowing orbs of its eyes remaining suspended in the darkness until they too disappear. Only then is the traveller safe to move on.

The black dog is not the only ghost on Winsford Hill. On its summit can be found the Caratacus Stone. This ancient standing stone has a simple inscription carved on it suggesting that it is a memorial to a descendant of the Iron Age chieftain Caratacus, who maintained a campaign of guerrilla warfare against the Romans in what is now North Wales and Shropshire. He was eventually captured and dragged off to Rome, where it was intended he would suffer public execution in the Colosseum. He was assumed by the Romans to be a

The ancient Tarr Steps are haunted by something very strange.
iStock

savage, but when he was brought before the Emperor and the Senate he surprised everyone by suddenly speaking Greek in the most courteous manner. Caratacus's life was spared and he was kept instead as a kind of curiosity in Rome, still a prisoner but well cared for.

The ghost of a man named Carter haunts the Caratacus Stone. Legend had it that a valuable treasure lay buried beneath the monolith and Carter decided to claim it for himself. In his attempt to unearth the gold, Carter dug around and undermined the stone, which toppled over and gave him such a smack in the head that he died on the spot. Ever since the desecration, the greedy fellow's spirit has been tied to the monument.

Arguably the wildest and least frequented section of Exmoor is a bleak, boggy area known as the Chains. In the 1800s the then owner of Exmoor, John Knight, decided to create a 30-foot-deep pond among the peat bogs, but no one seems to know why (my guess is he was simply extracting peat and the hole filled up with rainwater). Pinkery Pond is the rather pleasant name for this otherwise barren and forbidding place. Even a local walking guide refers to the pond as 'sinister'.
Pinkery Pond and the moors around it have a spooky reputation. The area is patrolled by a Grey Lady who has the unpleasant habit of leading travellers astray so that they fall into bogs. Phantom horsemen ride through the mists. Eerie blue lights have been seen hovering above the bogs. The lights may by marsh gas – or they may be something else.

The Tarr Steps is the name of a clapper bridge across the River Barle in Exmoor National Park. Clapper bridges are simple constructions of granite slabs laid over stone piers. The Tarr Steps are truly ancient, thought to date back to 1000 BC (although they have been restored and repaired continuously over the intervening millennia). The bridge's great antiquity worked on the popular imagination and tradition insisted that it had originally been built by the Devil himself.

Something strange and possibly as old as the bridge itself haunts the locality. A couple visiting the site saw what they described as 'the shape of a man, covered in hair' near the Tarr Steps. But this was no nudist holidaymaker, for only the upper half of the torso was visible: it floated about without any legs. The couple gawped at the grotesque apparition for a few seconds, and then it winked out of existence.

GLASTONBURY

Now world-famous for its rock festival, Glastonbury has been a magnet for pagans, occultists and other alternative thinkers for the best part of a century. This is because the town and the country round about is rich in folklore, much of it connected to King Arthur and to the fabulous Tor which rises so dramatically out of the Somerset Levels.

During the Middle Ages the monks of Glastonbury Abbey claimed they had discovered King Arthur's tomb, and that of his wife Guinevere, within their precincts. They immediately covered up the graves and refused to divulge where they had found them. Despite the total lack of evidence, this fishy yarn attracted thousands of pilgrims every year and swelled the abbey's coffers considerably.

An old engraving of Glastonbury showing the haunted George and Pilgrims Inn to the left.

There are a number of accounts of ghostly activity at Glastonbury Abbey. A member of the Ghost Club reported seeing a line of white-robed figures processing towards the Lady Chapel. He hurried after them, thinking that he might witness a quaint ceremony being performed, but once inside the ruined chapel, he was astonished to find no sign of the figures. He had only lost sight of them for a moment or two and there was nowhere for them to go. He found the Lady Chapel unnaturally quiet and possessed of an odd air of expectancy. There is also a report that the ruined abbey is haunted by a man whose dress and mode of speech suggests he dates from the Elizabethan period.

The former Abbey Grange, now Street House, also had a haunted reputation. During the closing years of the 19th century, a number of apparitions were observed, including a ghost dog, a nun, a 'little old man in a leathern jerkin' and a robed figure with an outstretched arm. In addition, an invisible horse and carriage would sometimes rattle up the drive.

In the centre of town can be found the wonderfully ancient George and Pilgrims Inn (now a hotel). The inn was built in the 15th century to house pilgrims to the abbey, as the name suggests. Its medieval origin has not been disguised over the centuries, thanks to its splendid stone frontage. One room in the hotel has long been haunted by a jolly, plump monk in a brown habit; every inch a Friar Tuck. The story to explain the ghost is that the monk hanged himself in the room, but this is at odds with his character. Not only is the monk always seen with a broad smile on his jovial countenance, he radiates an atmosphere of good cheer.

MINEHEAD

A popular seaside resort for Victorians, Minehead still has plenty of character and charm. For years Minehead was said to be haunted by the dreaded 'Mother Leakey', an indomitable individual whom many believed to have been a witch. Even on her death-bed (in 1634) she remained cantankerous. She told her daughter-in-law that she would return after death 'in the Devil's likeness'.

Initially, she appeared in no likeness at all, but disrupted the household with a fury of knocks, bangs, crashes and other noises. In one of the bedrooms there came a cacophony of sound like 'a drove of cattle' passing through. When Mother

Leakey's 14-year-old grandson lay dying of a long, debilitating disease, the unfortunate child claimed he could get no rest because of the constant appearances of his late grandmother in his room. After the boy died, a black mark was noticed on his throat which some thought resembled a hand-print.

Mother Leakey's daughter saw her apparition in her bedroom about a year after her death. According to a contemporary report, quoted by John Garland in his *Haunted Somerset*: 'She saw within her chamber, sitting in her chair, her mother in full proportion, and in her usual apparel, and being much astonished she beheld it a quarter of an hour but could not speak to it nor stir, and at last, it vanished away with a mighty groan.'

Minehead was the home of the wicked ghost of Mother Leakey, who would whistle up storms to sink ships. iStock

After that, Mother Leakey's ghost was frequently seen about the house and then she took to roaming around the town, bothering the townsfolk (on one occasion she kicked a doctor who had irritated her!). Her ghost was given to whistling wherever she roamed. Witches were believed to be able to 'whistle up' storms; for over a century, storms off Minehead were blamed on Mother Leakey's ghost, especially those which led to the foundering of ships.

Daniel Codd, in his *Mysterious Somerset and Bristol*, mentions an unusual incident which took place at Minehead in 1965. A number of people here saw a plane crash into the sea and a search and rescue operation was immediately carried out. No wreckage was found, however, and the witnesses later admitted there had been 'something abnormal' about the aircraft: it had appeared indistinct or misty.

MUCHELNEY

The ruined Benedictine Muchelney Abbey stands beside the attractive parish church of St Peter and St Paul. A fair proportion of the church is built from stone robbed from the abbey, which partly explains the latter's ruinous state. The Abbot's House is still standing, however. The whole complex is now managed by English Heritage.

In common with so many other old religious houses, Muchelney Abbey is said to be possessed of a phantom monk. Legend has it the monk had been a young nobleman forbidden by his father to marry the low-born girl he loved. Rather than marry for money, the youngster thwarted his family by taking holy orders at Muchelney. Some years later, he was astonished to meet his lost love again – and to discover that she too had sought comfort from her heartbreak by taking holy orders. She was now a nun. Their renewed love was too strong to deny and their forbidden relationship ended as tragically as one would expect. The unfortunate nun was walled up alive in her convent and the monk banished to some distant land (his noble status perhaps saving him from sentence of death).

The monk's form is seen making its way from the ruined cloisters to the Abbot's House. On occasions chanting in Latin has been heard emanating from the abbey site.

The Abbot's House at Muchelney Abbey, haunted by, appropriately enough, a phantom monk.

NUNNEY

The impressive shell of 14th-century Nunney Castle certainly looks as though it should have a ghost or two, but in fact it's the lane leading up to the castle that is reputedly haunted. The ghost hasn't been seen for a while but was very active in the 1970s.

In his *Ghosts of Today*, author Andrew Green explained: 'Several travellers have seen a man of about 35 wearing a sports jacket and flannel trousers standing beside the lane, hitching a lift. A number of motorists who have stopped to pick him up find that he has vanished. After waiting a few seconds for him to approach them, they have got out of their car to look for the stranger but he has completely disappeared.'

He adds: 'One or two friendly drivers have been so disturbed by the vanishing hiker that reports are filed with the local police. On more than one occasion the motorist claims to actually have had the man in the car with them, but he has vanished before reaching his destination of Critchill.'

A ghost in modern dress has hitched a lift in the lane leading past Nunney Castle.

PORLOCK

Porlock is an attractive village situated in a deep fold below Exmoor. Thanks to coastal changes it is now two miles from the sea, but is still possessed of the handsome little harbour called Porlock Weir. There are a number of haunted locations in and around Porlock, including its weir, where the hoofbeats of invisible horses have been heard and an ill-defined ghostly figure of a man has been glimpsed lurking by the stone steps.

Porlock Weir was formerly haunted by the ghost of a rowdy individual named Lucott, whose spirit did not lie easy in its grave and caused mayhem around the harbour. Twelve parsons were called in to exorcise the troublesome spook but only eleven showed up. Lucott laughed in their faces but was tricked by one of them into eating a consecrated wafer, at which point he was impelled to do what he was told. He mounted his spectral steed and galloped away into the afterlife, just pausing long enough to knock a gawping bystander's head so hard that his eye popped out. After that he troubled Porlock Weir no more.

Three men and a boy in antiquated clothing have been seen on the beach at Porlock Bay, making their way to a place called Marsh Field, where they vanish. They are thought to be the ghosts of sailors who were buried centuries ago in Marsh Field after their bodies were found washed up on the shingle after a storm.

Numerous spooks have been encountered on the hills above Porlock. Red Post Steep is patrolled after dark by an elegant phantom lady in a white gown with darker spots, who wears her hair in ringlets characteristic of the 17th century. She is seen striding down Old Lane to the site of a now demolished house.

Sparky

Porlock Weir, where a restless spirit had to be exorcised by a party of parsons. iStock

In addition Porlock Hill is haunted by a phantom hearse and the dismal cries of two soldiers who were hanged on its summit after the Battle of Sedgemoor (see below). 'Distant voices' are also a feature of Berry Castle, a local beauty spot which has an eerie reputation among ramblers, despite its charm. As well as the disembodied voices, many say they have suffered the uncomfortable sensation that they were being watched by unseen eyes.

SEDGEMOOR

The Battle of Sedgemoor is one of the most famous in English history. It was fought on July 6, 1685, and marked the end of the Monmouth Rebellion against the reign of King James II. As we have learnt in regards to Chard, James Scott, the First Duke of Monmouth, staged a coup to try to wrest the throne from the newly crowned James II. His short-lived rebellion was crushed by the king's army at Sedgemoor, near Westonzoyland. The Duke fled the battle but was soon captured and met his end on the block at the Tower of London.

Supernatural echoes of the brief but bloody Battle of Sedgemoor are said to have continued down the ages. Many people claim to have seen ghostly soldiers on the former battlefield, mainly in the vicinity of a dyke called the King's Drain. According to one source, the spooks sometimes appear as 'green blobs' floating above the field.

A man dressed in 'flowing white' and riding a white charger is thought to be the ghost of the Duke of Monmouth himself. The phantom tends to manifest on nights when the mist hangs low over the marsh. In years past people who live on the borders of Sedgemoor have heard hoofbeats thundering past their homes at breakneck speed. Although the horse and its rider are never seen, this too may be the ghost of the doomed Duke fleeing the scene when he realised it was all over.

The author Alasdair MacGregor briefly relates another spooky encounter on Sedgemoor in his book *Phantom Footsteps*. He was told that a couple named Robinson had been driving across Sedgemoor when 'they suddenly saw in front of them numbers of troopers strangely armed and as strangely attired'. The couple had passed away some years before MacGregor learnt of their encounter, but their son told him that his mother often used to mention it. 'As far as I remember,' said Mr Robinson, 'my mother cried out to my father to stop the car for fear of running into a number of people carrying staves and pikes.'

The King's Drain on Sedgemoor, where ghostly soldiers who died in the famous battle of 1685 are said to still be seen. Shutterstock/Stephen Rees

There is also a legend about one of the captured rebel soldiers being given a chance to win his freedom by a Royalist officer. He had been told that the young man was an exceptionally fast runner. Always ready for a wager, the officer bet him that if he could outrun a galloping horse ridden by one of the cavalrymen, his life would be spared and he would be free to go. Of course, the youth readily agreed to the challenge. Looking on anxiously was his sweetheart, who had followed him to the battle. The boy ran superbly and for a moment, it looked like he might outpace the horse – but then the Royalists shot him anyway. His girlfriend went mad with grief, and her distraught ghost is also said to haunt the battle site.

SHEPTON MALLET

Until its closure in 2013, HM Prison Shepton Mallet was the UK's oldest: it was founded in 1625. For many years the oldest parts of the gaol were believed to be haunted by the ghost of a woman who had been executed here. Because of the colour of her dress, she was known as the White Lady.

In the mid to late 1960s, however, the prison suddenly became very badly haunted. Both staff and prisoners told of hearing inexplicable bangs, thumps and a creepy sound like heavy breathing and of an atmosphere which was by turns oppressive and icy cold. A vague white shape – possibly the White Lady – was glimpsed in various parts of the building. One officer had an alarming experience when he attempted to lock a heavy door, only to feel someone or something pushing back at it from the other side. When he relinquished his grip, the door swung open to reveal – nothing.

In an attempt to quell the increasing talk of the prison being haunted, the governor himself decided to sleep in the duty room, the place that seemed to be most badly affected. He spent a restless night and reluctantly wrote to the Home Office that he was 'unable to find any satisfactory explanation for the happenings'.

As in so many cases, the haunting of Shepton Mallet Prison faded away on its own account, but odd noises and other spooky goings-on were still occasionally being reported as much as twenty years later. A new ghost was also spotted: a figure in the uniform of a Second World War GI. A section of the building had been used by the US Army during the war to imprison deserters or soldiers who had engaged in criminal activity. A few were executed, by Britain's last hangman, Albert Pierrepoint.

South of Shepton Mallet is Cannard's Grave, named after a publican-cum-highwayman who was hanged in chains opposite the inn he used to run. Giles or Tom Cannard (both names seem to be correct) was best known to his criminal chums as Tom the Taverner. Whenever a wealthy person came to the inn, or a merchant carrying valuable goods, Tom the Taverner would discreetly learn his guests' onward travel plans and then tip off the local footpads and highwaymen. Cannard would, of course, take his share of the proceeds of any robberies that subsequently took place. He would also allow his inn to be used as a hiding place or bolt-hole for any criminal who needed it.

The inn was situated on a crossroads of the busy Fosse Way and several other roads, which made it a convenient location for highway robbery. It was also considered a prominent place to erect a gibbet, and the bodies of felons were left dangling in chains directly opposite the pub. This grim view failed to deter Tom the Taverner from his criminal activities, however. Indeed, it is thought that after a time Cannard became dissatisfied with receiving just a small share of the profits and turned highwayman himself, with the inevitable result that in time it was his own body that was left swinging from the gibbet.

After his execution Cannard's ghost haunted his old inn and also the site of the gibbet. The pub no longer exists, but there's no reason to suppose that Cannard's ghost doesn't still lurk somewhere by the side of the road, poised to frighten travellers as it used to. Nowadays, however, modern vehicles pass by so quickly that maybe they are simply too fast for their passengers to notice him.

SOUTH CADBURY

Cadbury Castle is an ancient and mystical fortification on a hill which rises above the South Cadbury meadows. The hill has been occupied since the Stone Age and the fort encircling its summit dates back to the Bronze Age. Since at least the 17th century a legend has been recorded that King Arthur and his Knights of the Round Table lie sleeping under Cadbury Castle. Many believe the fort to have been the original Camelot.

Tradition states that Arthur and his knights ride out of the hill in spectral form once every seven years. They tend to favour bright moonlit nights for their excursions and a nice detail has it that their horses are shod with silver, so that the horseshoes glimmer as they pass. An Edwardian antiquarian notes that a

A splendid illustration by Gustave Doré of King Arthur and his knights. The legendary king and his company are said to still ride around the country near Cadbury Castle. iStock

genuine silver horseshoe was found in the vicinity of Cadbury Castle.

Nearby Sparkford is one of the spectral knights' favourite destinations after they have ridden out of Cadbury Castle. Here there was an ancient causeway which ran between two prehistoric burial mounds. King Arthur and company would ride along this causeway on Midsummer's Eve. Each of the knights would carry a spear, and each spear was tipped with flame. Sometimes only the flickering flames would be seen after dark, processing along the causeway.

STOGURSEY

Stogursey Castle is a fairy-tale sort of a place. Most of it is ruinous but it is romantically situated on an island ringed by a moat. Its 17th-century gatehouse survives intact and is reachable via a little stone bridge. The gatehouse has been restored by the Landmark Trust and is available as a holiday let. The castle was built by the Norman De Courcy family and its name is a corruption of Stoke Courcy.

During the first of his scraps with the Barons, King John used Stogursey Castle as a base of operations in Somerset. His ghost to said to still be seen riding about the fields near Stogursey, dressed as if for the hunt. 'Half-formed' figures have been glimpsed among the ruins and a phantom monk has been encountered in the castle roundhouse.

In the village itself, the Priory Church of St Andrew also has a haunted reputation. In a corner of its churchyard there stands the eerily named Dead House. This was used for a wide range of purposes in the past, from dispensing charity to storing bodies found washed up on nearby beaches. Visitors have reported being aware of an invisible presence in the Dead House and of unseen eyes watching them.

Not far away there is a Witch Tree, named after Harriet the Witch, a notorious village character of a previous century. Harriet is said to haunt the tree in the form of a fearsome black dog.

TAUNTON

Somerset's county town was an important Saxon settlement with its own mint, but the site has been inhabited since the Bronze Age. Its name means the 'town on the River Tone'. A wooden fort was erected here in AD 700, but after the Norman Conquest this was replaced by a stone castle. Taunton Castle found itself embroiled in the War of the Roses and a Cornish Uprising during the 15th century, and in the Civil War and the Monmouth Rebellion of the 17th century. Most of what survives today of the medieval castle is the heavily restored inner ward, which now houses two museums. Later extensions have been converted into a hotel.

After the failure of the Monmouth Rebellion, the ruthless 'Hanging' Judge Jeffreys was put in charge of prosecuting surviving rebels (see entries on Chard and Sedgemoor above). One of the most notorious of the so-called 'Bloody Assizes' that followed the Monmouth Rebellion was held within the Great Hall at Taunton Castle.

*aunton Castle has numerous ghosts, at least two of which recall the Bloody Assizes
f the 17th century.* *Alamy Picture Library*

The Great Hall (now used by the Somerset County Museum) is said to still resound to the sounds of marching feet, the echo of King James's soldiers as they brought forward more unfortunates to suffer under the judge's scorched-earth policy. Jeffreys himself is believed to haunt a landing in the castle: an imposing figure in red-and-white regalia and a long wig. He is also said to haunt the room he slept in during the Assizes at the 16th-century Tudor Tavern (now a coffee shop) in Fore Street.

A former curator of the Somerset County Museum reported two further ghosts in Taunton Castle. One of these was of a pretty young woman wearing the fashions of the 17th century. The other was more startling: a pair of clutching, disembodied hands. In addition, a grim-faced Cavalier brandishing both a sword and a pistol has been encountered on a stairway.

Attached to Taunton Castle is the Castle Hotel, which is haunted by the gentle presence of a lady violinist. The strains of a violin have been heard in one of the bedrooms, where a soft hand has also been felt stroking the bedclothes (hence the assumption that the violinist is female).

Just off the High Street can be found the Crescent, which boasts a street of elegant townhouses on one side and an ugly council block on the other. The apparition of an elderly lady in a long black dress, with black mittens on her hands, has been encountered pottering along the Crescent. She is believed to be Mrs Fitzherbert, who in her young and pretty days married the future George IV in a secret ceremony while he was still the Prince Regent.

The Wilton stream is said to be haunted by the ghost of a child who drowned in it. Rumour has it the drowning was not an accident.

WASHFORD

About a mile south-east of the village can be found Cleeve Abbey, a ruined monastery of the Cistercian order now in the care of English Heritage. Nearby Bardon House started life as the Abbey's grange and parts of it date back to the 13th century. It used to be the home of the important Leigh family and remains in private hands.

Many ghost stories are told about Bardon House. A headless black dog was said to manifest in the grounds as a spectral warning of an imminent death in the Leigh family. An Elizabethan ancestor, Robert Leigh, also haunts the house as a headless ghost, although Peter Underwood adds the amusing detail that the spectre is reputedly 'carrying round with him a head that was not his own'.

Another unusual ghost takes the form of a ghostly white dove. This is said to be the spirit of Mary, Queen of Scots. In 1836, according to tradition, a white dove shattered a window in an attic room and while this was being repaired, a bundle of 16th-century correspondence was discovered hidden in the eaves. These are now known as the 'Bardon Papers' and they consist of contemporary writings pertinent to the trial of Mary, Queen of Scots. Finally, there are reports of a carriage which is heard trundling up the drive to Bardon House but which is never seen.

WATCHET

An unlikely yarn is told about the parish church of this handsome harbour town. According to the story, a wealthy woman, Lady Florence Wyndham, had been interred in the crypt of St Decuman's Church and a gang of thieves were determined to help themselves to the valuable rings still worn on her dead fingers. On their way to the church they waylaid a passing schoolmaster and bullied him into showing them the way to the crypt. They then forced him to open Lady Florence's casket. However, 'the Dead' of the crypt immediately burst out of their own coffins and besieged the unfortunate schoolmaster and sent the would-be thieves fleeing.

The supposed truth behind this tale is scarcely less believable: that a greedy sexton removed the coffin lid and attempted to remove Lady Florence's rings, only to find that she was still alive. The tugging on her fingers woke her from a coma and she was reunited with her surprised but grateful family. Lady Florence's ghost is now said to haunt nearby Kentisford Farm. Dressed all in white, she is far from a gentle presence, for she has the unpleasant habit of shrieking in a spine-chilling manner.

Watchet's ghost train is not the seaside attraction you might expect, but the phantom of a steam engine which has been seen on the West Somerset Line after dark by numerous witnesses. Twenty miles of the West Somerset Line has been restored and steam trains are once again running along its scenic route to and from Minehead. However, the ghost train was first observed decades ago when the line had been taken up and the route was overgrown with weeds. It is described as

A steam train prepares to leave Watchet on the historic West Somerset Line. A not dissimilar ghost train has also been seen, and heard, on the line. iStock

being a locomotive pulling six mineral trucks. Sometimes only the eerie glow of its firebox is seen; at other times it remains invisible but can be heard passing down the line.

It is thought that the ghost might be linked to a fatal accident which occurred in 1857, when a mineral train returning from Minehead struck head-on a coal train steaming from Watchet. Three men lost their lives in the smash. In contrast to this tragedy, the sound of laughing children has also been heard on the line near Watchet station. This is thought to be the ghostly replay of Edwardian youngsters riding to their holidays.

Another form of transport, a ghostly galleon, is said to sail into Watchet Harbour, but it is believed to be a bad omen for anyone who sees it.

WELLS

Wells Cathedral, seat of the Bishop of Bath and Wells, is an Early Gothic masterpiece dating from the 12th and 13th centuries. The cathedral is particularly celebrated for the exceptional carvings of biblical figures on its West Front; for a wealth of surviving medieval stained glass; and for the so-called 'Sea of Steps' which leads up to the beautifully designed Chapter House.

In common with so many other ecclesiastical buildings, there are tales of phantom monks roaming around Wells Cathedral. In addition there are reports of the ghosts of plague victims haunting the Chapter House. The bodies of those who had succumbed to the Black Death were stored here in the early months of the outbreak in 1348.

In his book on *Haunted Houses*, published in 1956, Joseph Braddock writes: 'I possess a beautiful colour print of two ghostly figures on the steps going up to the Chapter House in Wells Cathedral. There are two figures – a small child and a much taller, perhaps maternal figure in white – standing framed in the archway at the entrance to the covered archway leading over the road to Vicars' Close.' The photo was taken by one of his friends, a Mr Hardy, on Easter Monday, 1954, on the aforementioned 'Sea of Steps'. He waited till there was no one around and then opened the shutter for fourteen seconds, watching all the time to make sure no one came into view. No one did, so the appearance on the negative of the adult and child mystified him completely. Unfortunately, Mr Braddock did not reproduce the photograph in his book and, so far as I know, it has never been published.

For many years the venerable King Charles Hotel in the High Street was haunted by a Cavalier. One of the witnesses was the young son of a former landlord, who described the apparition as 'a pretty man'! The Cavalier was usually seen on the back staircase and occasionally in the passageways to the rear of the building. Heavy footsteps were also heard on, or near, the staircase and were presumed to be made by the Cavalier stomping about. He may also have been responsible for the strains of a harpsichord which drifted from no fixed point. The King Charles Hotel ceased to be a hostelry some time ago and is currently a toyshop. There are no reports as yet of the 'pretty man' being observed by any of its young clientele.

number of ghosts haunt the magnificent Wells Cathedral, especially in or near the Chapter House. iStock

WESTON-SUPER-MARE

The old Queen Alexandra Memorial Hospital on the Boulevard in this popular seaside town was haunted by a nurse in a blue uniform. She would visit the wards at night and was known to speak to patients, going so far as to discuss their illnesses with them.

One patient described seeing a woman in a long blue dressing gown entering the ward where she was lying sleepless one night. Despite the similar colour of their outfits, this must be a different ghost, for it approached the patient's bed and the witness got a clear look at it. At first she assumed it was a patient who had strayed from another ward, but as the figure got closer to the bed, the witness suddenly felt terrified, for reasons she couldn't have explained. However, the figure in the blue gown seemed to notice this and it backed away. Then it walked straight through a closed door! Something had instinctively warned the witness there was something unearthly about the stranger.

Very unusual apparitions have been reported from the town's Victorian park. In the area known as The Shrubbery, great shambling black shadows have been observed bumbling through a dip between the bushes. When encountered, dog-walkers have reported their pets' growling responses to the bulky phantoms. They are thought to be the apparitions of bears formerly kept in a menagerie at a nearby mansion.

WOOKEY HOLE

A short distance from Wells can be found one of Somerset's most enduring tourist attractions: Wookey Hole Caves. The caverns consist of a long series of dry chambers and a further series of submerged caves which are only accessible to divers. All the caves have resulted from the erosion of limestone by rainwater and by the River Axe which flows through them. Wookey Hole Caves have been lived in for 45,000 years, since the Old Stone Age, and almost consistently thereafter. In 2009 a resident 'witch' was hired to live on-site to help attract and entertain the thousands of visitors who flock to the caverns every year.

The 'Witch of Wookey' features strongly in Somerset folklore. At first a pure-hearted girl, she was jilted in love, and bitterness poisoned her soul. She became consumed with jealous hatred for all young lovers and, retreating to the damp darkness of Wookey Hole Caves, practised the dark arts, dooming every lover who crossed her path to a failed relationship. One young man whom she cursed in this way joined a monastery at Glastonbury in order to forget his disappointment. In holy orders his faith grew stronger, and he determined that the Witch of Wookey should be prevented from spoiling any more lives.

The vengeful monk made his way to the caverns and there called upon the witch to come out and face him. Recognising that the tables had been turned, the witch retreated into the darkness of her cave, but the monk pursued her and, scooping up some water from the River Axe, dribbled it over her head while seeking a blessing from God to end her wickedness. Instantly, the witch was turned to stone. The 'Witch of

Wookey' can still be seen today, a tall stalagmite in the first chamber of the caverns. The skeleton of a woman, over a thousand years old, was found in the cavern in 1912, and inevitably this too was pronounced to be the remains of the witch. There are persistent stories that the Witch of Wookey now haunts the caves where she once lived.

Other strange phenomena have also been reported by speleologists exploring the deeper caves. In one pot-hole that had remained blocked by gravel for centuries, they heard inexplicable tapping noises and a sound as though someone was dragging themselves painfully through the tunnel.

Peculiar things also occurred when a television crew were filming episodes of *Doctor Who* in Wookey Hole Caverns in 1975. Several technicians reported glimpsing shadowy figures in the caves that they initially took to be members of the cast.

Two of those cast members, Elisabeth Sladen and Ian Marter (now both sadly deceased), had a particularly puzzling experience. Ms Sladen explained that there was a scene in her script of *Revenge of the Cybermen* which she didn't much like nor fully understand. It was a scene she shared with Ian Marter, and when she raised her concerns with him, he agreed that he felt much the same about it. The next day they took their copies of the script to the director, Michael Briant, to gain some insight into the troubling scene, only to discover that he had no knowledge of it. The two actors checked their scripts – and found that the scene they had both individually read was no longer in either of their copies. The page was blank and neither of them could remember the dialogue that had so puzzled them.

Tradition states this stalagmite in Wookey Hole Caverns is a witch who has been turned to stone.

Michael Briant and his wife had an even spookier experience. Before filming began, Mr Briant was given permission to scout out the caverns for location shoots. Because he was likely to spend a good many hours exploring the caves and might not be finished before midnight, he was locked in by a caretaker and given a key to let himself out when he was ready. His wife decided to accompany him. In an interview with the blog site drwhointerviews.wordpress.com, Mr Briant explained what happened next:

'With my wife, I duly set off into the caverns and after about two hours of wandering about, taking notes, somebody came up. I thought at first he was a security guy but then I saw he was dressed in a wet suit. I asked him how he had got in and he said, "Oh, I always come in. Can I borrow your torch?"

'I refused because I needed it to see with, and the man said, "Right you are," before going off into the gloom. Shortly afterwards, we heard a little Irish tune whistling from the shadows and both my wife and I began to feel a bit scared. I decided to call it a night, even though I hadn't finished, but first I asked the caretaker who the man had been and why he had been let in. I was told: "We didn't let anyone in. He was an Irishman who died down there pot-holing, three years ago." Of course I couldn't tell anyone, because my film unit would never have worked there.'

YEOVIL

The Elephant & Castle is a former Victorian hotel on the corner of Lower Middle Street and Wyndham Street. It opened in 1860 but two years later tragedy struck when its first landlord, Job Osment, threw himself out of his top-storey bedroom window in the small hours of April Fool's Day. At the subsequent inquest, his wife and father-in-law explained that Job 'had appeared very strange in his manner for the past two months'. His wife was woken by him climbing out of the window and had managed to grab his legs. But she wasn't strong enough to hold him. Job plummeted to the ground and died of his injuries some days later.

This tragedy may be linked to the haunting of the Elephant & Castle, although the ghost seen here is of a woman, not a man. She is described as wearing a long white gown and carrying either a lamp or a candle. She has some sort of head-dress that obscures her face. Could it perhaps be the ghost of the distraught Mrs Osment, in her nightgown, hurrying to help her unfortunate husband?

One landlady was convinced the ghost is that of a former maid, however. One of her reasons for thinking so was that in the middle of the night she would often hear sounds like crockery and cutlery being stacked, although nothing was ever found to be out of place the next morning.